SCHUMANN

FANTASIESTÜCKE
(Fantasy Pieces)

OPUS 12
FOR THE PIANO

EDITED BY MAURICE HINSON

AN ALFRED MASTERWORK EDITION

Alfred

Copyright © MCMXCII by Alfred Publishing Co., Inc.
All rights reserved. Printed in USA.

Cover art: Golden Autumn, *1895*
by Isaac Levitan (1860–1900)
Tretyakov Gallery, Moscow, Russia
Scala/Art Resource, New York

ROBERT SCHUMANN
Fantasiestücke (Fantasy Pieces), Op. 12

Maurice Hinson, Editor

CONTENTS

This edition is dedicated to
Dr. and Mrs. Louis Ball
with admiration and
appreciation.

Maurice Hinson

Foreword

Robert Schumann's piano compositions of the 1830s are works of great originality, creativity and innovation. Their bold harmonies, surprising modulations, unusual rhythms and distinct melodic charm greatly intrigued Schumann's contemporaries. Schumann's approach to musical composition was largely poetic. In his early teens, he focused more on poetry than music. During this time, he began work on a novel. He also wrote poems, sketches and dramas. He emulated authors such as Jean Paul (Johann Paul Friedrich Richter, 1763–1825) and E.T.A. Hoffmann (1776–1822). Their influence guided Schumann for many years and provided a model for several of his compositions.

Schumann was aware of the split in his artistic personality. While composing *Papillons*, Op. 2 (1829–31), he exclaimed to his mother: "I wish I would be all in something and not what I, unfortunately, have always been, something in everything." Despite his misgivings, it was precisely his poetic talent which generated a unique series of piano works. These compositions are extraordinary piano cycles with titles such as *Papillons* (butterflies—inspired by Jean Paul's novel *Die Flegeljahre*), *Davidsbündlertanze*, *Carnaval* (subtitled *Scènes mignonnes sur quatre notes*), *Fantasiestücke* and *Kreisleriana*. The spiritual, poetic qualities contained in all these works have their roots in the novels of Jean Paul.

Background

The *Fantasiestücke* (Fantasy Pieces) were composed in the spring of 1837 when Schumann was separated from his fiancée, Clara Wieck. *Carnaval*, published in 1837, and *Fantasiestücke*, published in 1838, were the first piano works in which Schumann used titles for each individual movement. Schumann repeatedly stated that these programmatic titles were given to the compositions only *after* their completion. The titles reflect Schumann's changeable moods during this time. Schumann dedicated the set to the Scottish pianist Anna Robena Laidlaw, who was performing in Leipzig that year. Musically, however, it was addressed to Clara. The 18-year-old Laidlaw, it is said, may have temporarily subdued Schumann's ardent pursuit of Clara.

Schumann submitted the *Fantasiestücke* to Breitkopf & Härtel, who published it in February 1838.

Despite the fact that much of his music was too advanced for many listeners of his day, Schumann nevertheless felt that at least two of the *Fantasiestücke* could become popular. In a letter to Clara dated December 22, 1837, he wrote:

> None of my things will really do for playing in public, but among the *Fantasiestücke* there is one, *In der Nacht* and another, *Traumeswirren*; they will be published soon, then just look at them.

A few months later he wavered:

> I should think you might play *Traumeswirren* and *Des Abends* in public some day. I fancy that *In der Nacht* is too long.

Then on April 21, 1838, Schumann wrote an interesting letter to Clara in which he dwells on *In der Nacht*. How Schumannesque it all is! He writes that a mutual friend considers *In der Nacht* the best piece in the *Fantasiestücke*,

> and I think it is mine too. After I had finished it I found, to my delight, that it contained the story of Hero and Leander. Of course you know it: how Leander swam every night through the sea to his love, who awaited him at the beacon and showed him the way with a lighted torch. It is a beautiful, romantic old story. When I am playing *In der Nacht* I cannot get rid of the idea; first he throws himself into the sea; she calls him; he answers; he battles with the waves and reaches land in safety. Then the Cantilena, when they are clasped in one another's arms, until they have to part again, and he cannot tear himself away until night wraps everything in

darkness once more. Do tell me if the music suggests the same thing to you.[1]

It is important to remember that Schumann superimposed this romantic story upon the music after he had finished composing it. There is no limit to the fictional descriptive patterns that can be draped over a musical composition. But they are all private, arbitrary and self-oriented. It is highly unlikely that anyone but Schumann would have derived from *In der Nacht* the story of Hero and Leander. He was ever the romantic.

In an April 1838 letter to his friend Carl Kragen, Schumann remarked: "Liszt, who is in Vienna, is said to have sightread the *Fantasiestücke* to the delight of everyone; the *Ende vom Lied* in particular." On March 13, 1838, he wrote to Clara about *Ende vom Lied*:

> I thought that, now I had reached the end, everything would resolve itself in a merry wedding. But as I thought of you, sorrow came over me, and the result was a chime of wedding bells mingled with a death knell.

Like its joyous march that suddenly melts into a pianissimo coda, *Ende vom Lied* could be an image of Schumann's whole life.

Schumann borrowed the title *Fantasiestücke* from E.T.A. Hoffmann (1776–1882), whose *Fantasiestücke in Callots Manier* combined stories and sketches on music and musicians. Hoffmann's composition is fanciful but penetrating; at times, even disturbing.

About This Edition

This edition is based on the original published in February 1838 by Breitkopf & Härtel in Leipzig, plate number 5835, a and b. Also available for reference was Johannes Brahms's copy of the first edition. Brahms added a number of corrections which had already been included in the complete edition of Schumann's works, edited by Clara Schumann (*Phantasiestücke*, 1879). Schumann's pedal indications are identified in footnotes; all other pedal marks are editorial. More or less pedal than indicated may be used. Schumann's fingerings are printed in italics; all other fingerings, as well as parenthetical material, are editorial.

Sources Consulted in the Preparation of This Edition

I wish to thank the authors and editors of the works quoted in this collection:

Abraham, Gerald, ed. *Schumann: A Symposium*. London: Oxford University Press, 1952.

Chissel, Joan. *Schumann Piano Music*. London: British Broadcasting Corp., 1972.

Ostwald, Peter. *Schumann: The Inner Voices of a Musical Genius*. Boston: Northeastern University Press, 1985.

Schumann, Robert. *Jugendbriefe* 2d ed.; edited by Clara Schumann. Leipzig: Breitkopf & Härtel, 1904.

Taylor, Ronald. *Robert Schumann: His Life and Works*. New York: Universe Books, 1982.

About the Music

There is no mistaking the programmatic intentions of this famous set of pieces. The titles served simply as a guide to interpretation and performance. Schumann's titles correspond perfectly with the musical content. As a result, the titles and the music have long been indissolubly connected in the minds of interpreters.

The formal structure of the *Fantasiestücke* are more complex that that of any of their predecessors. Their pianistic layout is more varied: no two pieces are alike in shape, style or mood. They are flights of fancy, as their titles indicate. The *Fantasiestücke* were originally issued in two sets of four each. Their internal structure is designed so that each of the four opening pieces in the first part is perfectly balanced against the four in the second part. The titles of the two sections are arranged around contrasting tonalities. In the first section, they are arranged around D-flat major, representing the real world. Those in the second part focus mainly around the tonality of F, representing Schumann's fantasy world.

The remarkable symmetry of this work demonstrates not only Schumann's creative originality but also his desire to appeal to Clara. "You want everything [in art] to be stormy all the time, with flashes of lightning, as though it's all new and has never happened before," he wrote her. "But there are also old and eternal states that control us." Clara came to love the *Fantasiestücke* and performed them frequently, with great success.

Although these eight pieces form a homogeneous whole, each can be played individually without serious loss of effect. We clearly hear "Clara's theme" in the opening measures of *Des Abends*:

(Des Abends)

measures 2–5

"Clara's theme" is also heard in the opening measures of *Warum?* and *Grillen*:

(*Warum?*)   (*Grillen*)

measures 1–3   measures 1–2

The "Clara theme" recurs throughout the cycle; it reappears in an inverted form in secondary themes throughout in, for example, *Des Abends*, *Aufschwung* and *Grillen*.

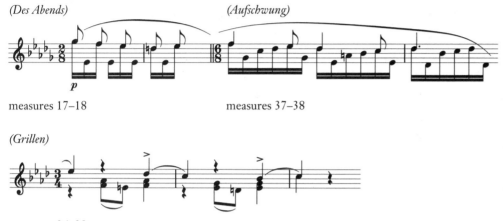

(*Des Abends*)   (*Aufschwung*)

measures 17–18   measures 37–38

(*Grillen*)

measures 26–28

1. *Des Abends* (Evening)

This piece opens with Clara's keynote theme, the familiar descending scale heard throughout his piano sonatas. Here it is embedded in a restless triplet rhythm. The opening character directions, *sehr innig zu spielen* (to be played very inwardly, intimately), provide the key to a beautiful performance. The lyrical and gentle opening melody is worked into a flowing, broken-chord accompaniment. A Schumannesque rhythmic device is employed, in which duple meter (2/8) is made to sound like triple (3/8).

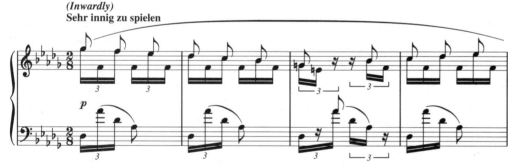

measures 1–4

To preserve the 2/8 meter, the left-hand triplet movement must be strictly maintained. Avoid extensive rubatos in the melody. The indicated fingerings make possible an unbroken legato. In measure 6, play the grace notes ahead of the beat.

A bold plunge from D-flat major to E major takes place at measure 25. This sweet piece is monothematic, its second half (measures 39–76) being an exact repetition of the first, followed by a brief coda (measure 77 to the end). The last note of the right hand (measure 88) should sound like a distant bell. Subtle contrasts, smooth phrasing and poetic sensitivity are required throughout. The piece creates a perfect impression of a quiet evening: nature at rest.

Form: **A A¹ A A¹** coda. (Part I) **A** = measures 1–16; **A¹** = 17–38; (Part I repeated) **A** = 39–54; **A¹** = 55–76; coda = 77–88.

2. *Aufschwung* (Soaring)

In this exhilarating virtuoso piece Schumann uses the full resources of modern piano technique. Numerous cross rhythms, as well as harmonic and melodic counterpoint, serve to bring out the contrasting melodies. Skillful playing is required for octaves in uncomfortable positions. Good chord and figuration playing are also essential. Strive for a lyrical tone and an imaginative approach. The piece represents Schumann's attempts to express inner mood; it is a quintessential Florestanian (impetuous, energetic, determined) character piece.

A good right-hand 10th is desirable, but for those with smaller hands, the following might be helpful:

measures 1–3

And in parallel passages:

measure 114

and:

measure 147

Practice measures 93–103 with special attention to the opposing dynamic marks in the right and left hands. Schumann did not include a poco ritard at the final cadence, but these measures (153–154) will not sound affirmative enough without it.

Form: Sectional, **A B A C A B A**. **A** = measures 1–16; **B** = 16–40; **A** = 40–52; **C** = 53–114; **A** = 114–122; **B** = 122–146; **A** = 146–154. The form may be considered sonata-rondo, but the conception of mood involves thematic recurrence and contrast rather than development.

3. *Warum?* (Why?) 20

A short but compelling melodic fragment dominates Eusebius's gentle, questioning, "Why?" Eusebius represents the gentle, longing side of Schumann's personality while Florestan represents his impetuous, excitable characteristics. Florestan and Eusebius were two of the charter members of the *Davidsbund* (League of David), which existed largely in Schumann's mind. Schumann mentioned the *Davidsbund* in two essays published in *Der Komet* (The Comet) in 1833. The *Davidsbund* members stood for the highest ideals in music and were united against the Philistines, who were the reactionary, uncultivated enemies, representing the current vogue of virtuosity. The lyricism of this piece makes it a "Song without Words" similar to those of Mendelssohn. The melodic fragment floats over a syncopated accompaniment, leaving open the ends of the four-measure periods in expectation of an answer that never comes. In measure 10, play the two grace notes before the beat. The ethereal arpeggio grace notes of measure 13 should be played ahead of the beat. The *p* in this measure should be played subito. The grace notes should sound as though melted into the line. Make a big ritard at measure 30. This ritard applies to the second quarter note (left hand) only. Play the repeat, and add an extensive rallentando to the final phrase. This refined piece is filled with a hesitant charm, necessitating subtle nuances in the voicings. Also needed throughout the work is a good sense of rubato.

Form: **A B** Variation on **A**. **A** = measures 1–16; **B** = 17–30; Variation on **A** = 31–42.

4. *Grillen* (Whims) 22

Emphasis on the linear forward motion will prevent the ponderous, bombastic quality that often mars this energetic work. It requires good chord playing; large hands are helpful for performing this capricious, funny piece. Measures 1–8 are marked *mf* at the beginning but always *f* thereafter when this section returns; however, the *f* should always be treated carefully, not too loud. The **C** section (measures 60–97) features a rhythmic syncopation typical of Schumann. This offers a welcome contrast to the buoyant vitality of the surrounding material. Section **C**'s shifting stresses and accents can be made clear only with very rhythmical playing. Despite the opening short staccato chords, the top melody line should be easy for the listener to discern. An analysis of measure 15 shows that only the outer voices (of the fast-moving three chords) move in octaves. There is humor in this darting, fanciful piece. An imaginative performance depends greatly upon a variety of colorful touches, including staccato, portato and accents.

Form: Sonata-rondo, **A B A C A B A**. **A** = measures 1–16; **B** = 16–44; **A** = 44–60; **C** = 60–97; **A** = 97–113; **B** = 113–141; **A** = 141–157.

5. *In der Nacht* (In the Night) 26

This turbulent piece (Schumann's favorite of the set) is not a nocturne but a ghost story. The unceasingly agitated 16th notes are important to the interpretation. They form a background to the violent melodic outbursts that punctuate the work. Finger independence is necessary throughout. The lyrical middle section (measures 69–143) contains melodic material that soars above the mass of accompanimental textures: the 16th notes must flow evenly. Dynamic contrasts should not be exaggerated. Only two places are marked *ff*: the return of the main idea at measures 138–141, and the closing measures (210–212). Schumann's fingerings in measures 11–12 require agility but are very effective. Do not accelerate measure 108: the tension produced by the crescendo is intensified if the slower tempo is maintained. Return to Tempo I at measure 109. The canonic treatment of measures 122–129 should be kept in strict tempo. After the accelerando (measures 130–139), resume the original tempo at measure 140. In the closing measures (218 to the end), no stringendo is needed to intensify the unrelenting drive towards the end. The perpetual-motion figuration and the many cross rhythms make this chromatic night mystery one of the most difficult of the *Fantasiestücke*.

Form: **A B A** coda. **A** = measures 1–68; **B** = 69–143; **A** = 144–205; coda = 206–223.

6. *Fabel* (Fable) 34

The clear C major harmonies and vivid narratives of this piece provide relief after the whirling, chromatic breathlessness of *In der Nacht*. Both the dreamy *Langsam* and the alternating staccato *Schnell* sections enhance this effect. This piece is scherzolike without being merry. The wistful, quiet manner with which the music begins and ends is the true essence of this piece. The exact tempo ratio in the Clara Schumann edition "Slow (♩ = 48) — Fast (♩ = 48)" effectively maintains musical coherency. The sectional nature of this piece and its many fermatas will best be served by a constant forward momentum. The fermata should lengthen the note values by about half as much again. Schumann's careful notation of articulation should be studied thoroughly.

Form: **A B A¹ B¹ C B A²** (coda). **A** = measures 1–4; **B** = 4–12; **A¹** = 13–20; **B¹** = 20–28; **C** = 29–69; **B** = 70–77; **A²** (coda) = 78–89.

7. *Traumes Wirren* (Dream Confusion) 38

The title can also be translated, "Dream Visions," "Restless Dreamer," "Restless Dreams" and "Disturbing Dreams." This difficult piece scurries by in breathless fashion; play it with great liveliness. A fully developed technique is essential as are sensitivity and tastefulness. A fine rotational technique and strong outer fingers will help manage the swirling 16th notes, and keep the piece dancing along. One exception is measures 63–94, in which flowing quarter notes are played molto legato and without rubato. Of all the *Fantasiestücke*, Schumann considered this movement and *Des Abends* (No. 1) to be the most suitable for Clara to perform for her more conservative audiences. Avoid making *Traumes Wirren* sound like a study by skillfully stressing the melodic flow. Begin quietly. The fingerings for the opening 16th-note figuration may deviate from those suggested depending on the size and shape of the hand. When crossing hands, the left hand always goes over the right. Heighten the whimsical and fantastic character of *Traumes Wirren* with an extremely delicate approach.

Form: **A B A** coda. **A** = measures 1–62; **B** = 63–122; **A** = 123–170; coda = 171–177.

8. *Ende vom Lied* (The End of the Song) 45

The title could also be translated, "The End of the Story." In accordance with its title, this piece sums up or rounds off the *Fantasiestücke*. It is therefore best performed when the complete cycle is played. The indication *Mit gutem Humor* ("with good humor") precludes any suggestion of pathos in musical interpretation. The piece reflects the bright freshness of early youth. Although it consists of many chords requiring hand and arm technique, a thick sonority should be avoided. Use a light articulation for the accented notes on the weak beats of the measure (measures 4, 8, 10, 12, 14–16, etc.). Schumann's pedal indication at measures 85–94 cannot be followed literally. Half-pedal will better serve the sonority so that pedal changes between two-measure groups can be somewhat disguised. The more lively **B** section (measures 24–60) borrows a melodic and rhythmic motive from the opening and closing movements of *Carnaval*, Op. 9. Strike the repeated chords firmly but not bombastically. The spirited opening material returns in measure 61. This is followed by a quiet, reflective coda (measure 85) based on the main theme, ending the *Fantasiestücke* on a note of blissful calm.

Form: **A B A** coda. **A** = measures 1–24; **B** = 24–60; **A** = 60–84; coda = 85–117.

Fantasiestücke
(Fantasy Pieces)
1837

Des Abends
(Evening)

Op. 12

(a) Schumann indicated pedal in measure 1, first beat; up at measure 37 on the fourth 16th note; pedal down at measure 39, first beat; up at measure 75 on the fourth 16th note; pedal down at measure 77, first beat. His pedal marks mean the pedal should be used at the performer's discretion during these sections as opposed to being held down until the release sign; sometimes there is no release sign.

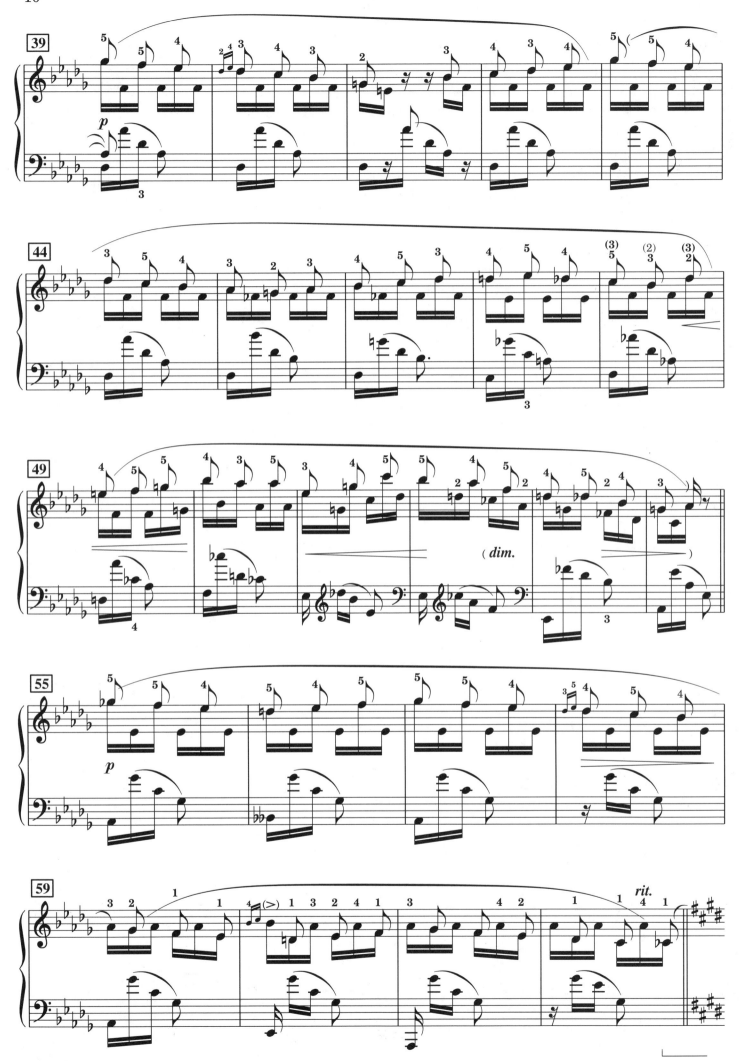

9

Aufschwung
(Soaring)

(a) Schumann's only pedal mark is a *p* at the beginning of the piece; in measure 83, pedal down on count 1 and up on count 6, and in measure 115, pedal down on count 1.

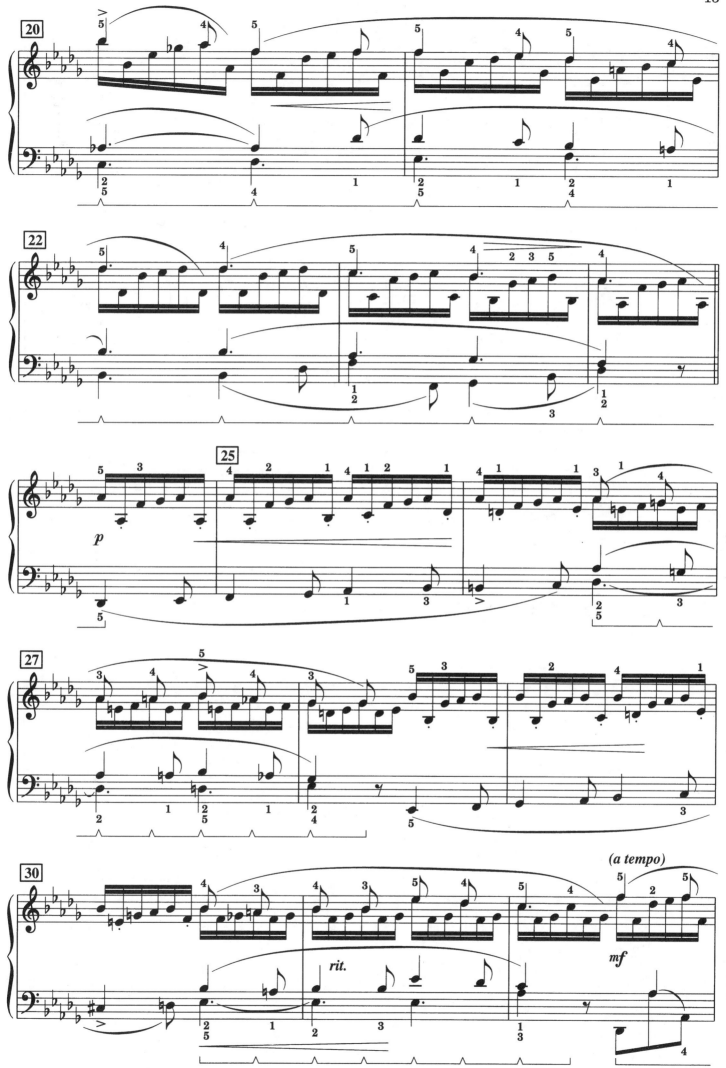

(b) Fingerings in italics are from the original edition.

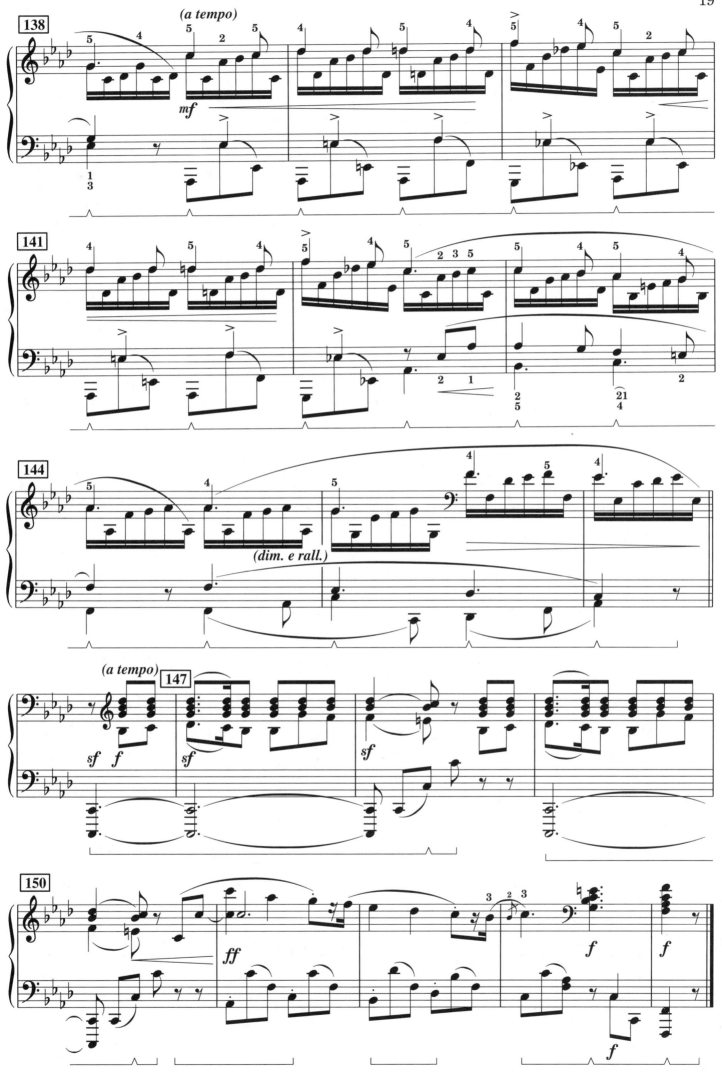

Warum?
(Why?)

(Slowly and tenderly ♩ = ca. 58)
Langsam und zart

ⓐ Schumann indicated pedal at measures 1, 13 and 31.

ⓑ

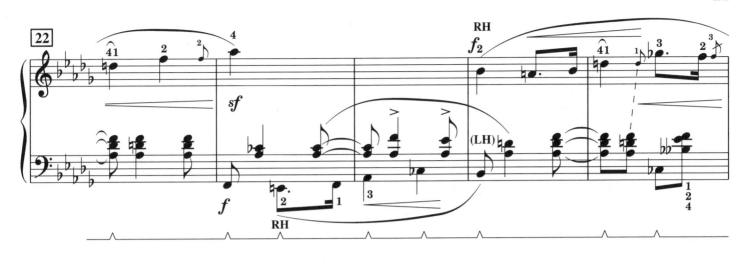

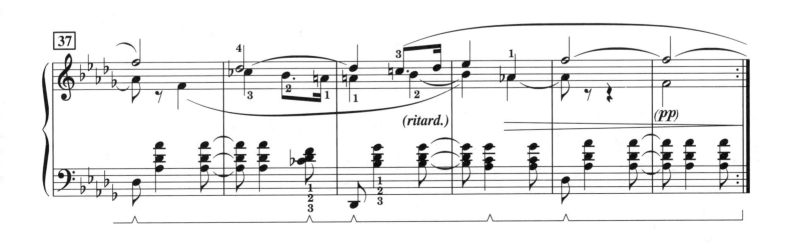

Grillen
(Whims)

(a) Schumann indicates pedal only on the first chord.

24

25

In der Nacht
(In the Night)

(With passion ♩ = ca. 116)
Mit Leidenschaft

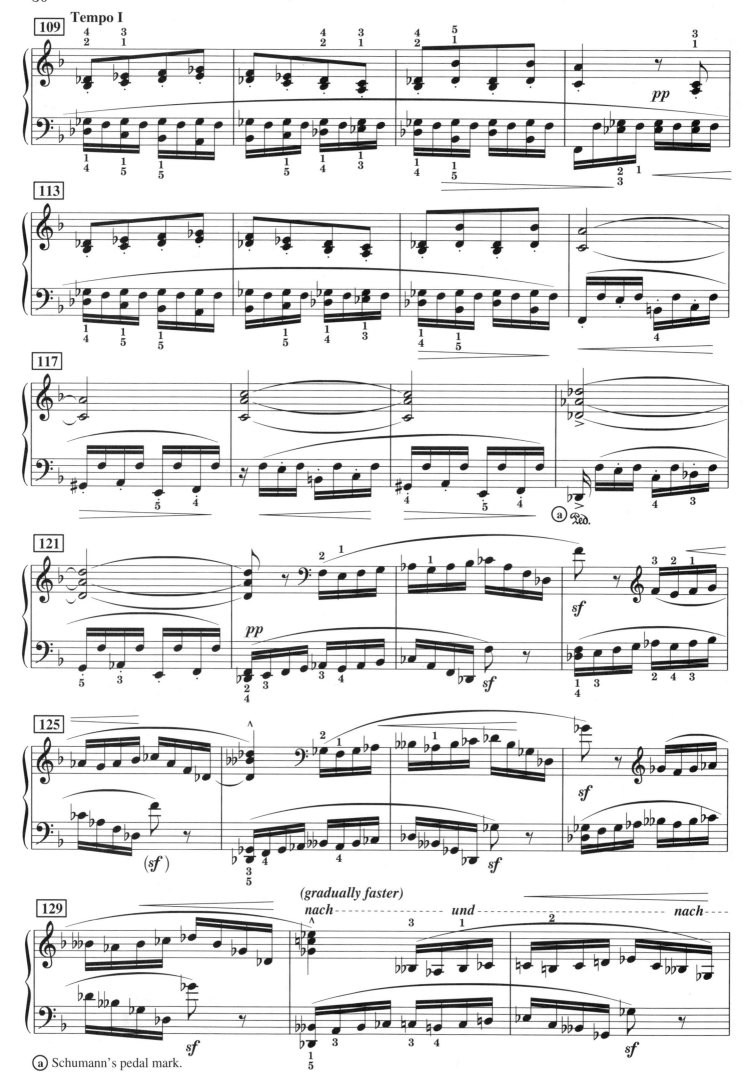

a Schumann's pedal mark.

222222

2222

2222

22222222

Fabel
(Fable)

ⓐ Schumann's pedal mark.

Traumes Wirren
(Dream Confusion)

(a) Schumann's pedal mark.

(b) Schumann's pedal mark.

Ende vom Lied
(The End of the Song)

ⓐ Schumann's pedal marks.

48